Cheese

FOR

DUMMIES®

MINI EDITION

by *Culture Magazine*,
Laurel Miller and
Thalassa Skinner

WILEY

John Wiley & Sons Canada, Ltd.

Cheese For Dummies® Mini Edition

Published by
John Wiley & Sons Canada, Ltd.
6045 Freemont Boulevard
Mississauga, Ontario, L5R 4J3
www.wiley.com

For details on how to create a custom book for your company or organization, or for more information on John Wiley & Sons Canada custom publishing programs, please call 416-646-7992 or e-mail cupubcan@wiley.com.

For general information on John Wiley & Sons Canada, Ltd., including all books published by Wiley Publishing, Inc., please call our warehouse, Tel 1-800-567-4797. For reseller information, including discounts and premium sales, please call our sales department, Tel 416-646-7992. For press review copies, author interviews, or other publicity information, please contact our marketing department, Tel 416-646-4584, Fax 416-236-4448.

ISBN: 978-1-118-06164-0

Printed in the United States

1 2 3 4 5 DP 15 14 13 12 11

Publisher's Acknowledgements

We're proud of this book; please send us your comments at
http://dummies.custhelp.com.

Some of the people who helped bring this book to market include
the following:

Acquisitions and Editorial

Acquiring Editor:
Robert Hickey

Manager, Custom Publications:
Christiane Coté

Production Editor:
Lindsay Humphreys

Composition Services

Production Coordinator:
Kristie Rees

Layout: Claudia Bell,
Lavonne Roberts

Proofreader: Robert Springer

John Wiley & Sons Canada, Ltd.

Deborah Barton, Vice President and Director of Operations

Karen Bryan, Vice-President, Publishing Services

Jennifer Smith, Publisher, Professional and Trade Division

Alison Maclean, Managing Editor

Publishing and Editorial for Consumer Dummies

Diane Graves Steele, Vice President and Publisher,
Consumer Dummies

Kristin Ferguson-Wagstaffe, Product Development Director,
Consumer Dummies

Ensley Eikenburg, Associate Publisher, Travel

Kelly Regan, Editorial Director, Travel

Composition Services

Debbie Stailey, Director of Composition Services

Contents at a Glance

Introduction

• •

Cheese has been around for thousands of years, but it has only recently come into the spotlight in the United States. A growing number of cheese shops are opening across the country, and supermarkets are selling a much wider selection of cheeses — both domestic and import.

But with so many kinds of cheese available, how do you know what's to your liking? We're complete cheese geeks, but we understand that learning about cheese, like wine, can be confusing, overwhelming, and (in the wrong hands) pretentious. Our goal is to demystify cheese — which is, after all, mostly milk — and help you feel comfortable with buying, tasting, and serving it.

Icons Used in This Book

We use the following icons in this book:

This icon highlights any wisdom we have to offer about how to buy, serve, or store cheese.

When you see this icon, we're telling you essential cheese information. This is the stuff that you need to know.

This is the stuff you don't need to know. It's technical information that we find fascinating, but our feelings won't be too hurt if you don't feel the same. Just think of it as great trivia, or a way to impress and educate your friends over a plate of (what else?) cheese.

You didn't think we'd leave you hanging, did you? This icon indicates how to best serve or pair a cheese with other foods or beverages, or what applications (cooking, melting, or snacking) are best for a cheese.

Where to Go from Here

This minibook is a reference guide, structured so that each chapter or section stands on its own. If you just want to know how to make a delectable cheese plate or beverage pairing for your next party, head to Chapter 4. Chapters 2 and 3 break down the different styles of soft and hard cheeses, and provide you with serving suggestions for each. If you want to learn about how cheese is made — from the animal to the plate — Chapter 1 will take you there.

Chapter 1

Cheese 101

In This Chapter

▶ Exploring how cheese is made

▶ Examining what determines a cheese's style

*I*t's hard to believe that something as complex, delicious, and downright diverse as cheese is made of just a few key ingredients. Thousands of types of cheese are made around the world — from the milk of cows, goats, sheep, water buffalo, yak, and camels (even reindeer, donkeys, and horses!). Depending on the country, this ancient food can hold significant cultural or nutritive value.

In this chapter, we explore the basics of cheesemaking, starting with its key component, milk, and move on to what makes one cheese's *style* (the various categories of cheese, depending on age, moisture content, texture, and rind) different from another.

Making Cheese

The cheesemaking process has changed little over the centuries, despite increased knowledge about microbiology and chemistry. The cheesemaker is, in essence, like a chef, with a multitude of recipes at his or her fingertips. However, the cheesemaker's most important decision is what type of milk to use and then to ensure that the milk is of the highest quality.

Milk matters

Milk is such a commonplace food. It's white, fluid, and with the exception of fat content, most folks don't give it much thought. Yet it's an incredibly complex liquid, with seasonal and chemical variations depending on the species of animal it comes from.

Here are the main components in milk that provide the most critical factors in cheesemaking:

- ✔ **Butterfat:** Also known as *milk fat*, this is the natural fatty constituent of milk and the chief component of butter. Clarified butter is milk fat without water or liquid.

- ✔ **Casein:** Pronounced "cay-seen," this is the main protein in milk and is, together with butterfat, what becomes the solids (*curds*) when milk is coagulated to make cheese.

The three main milks used in cheesemaking are cow, goat, and sheep. Each has its own characteristics in terms of flavor, color, and texture.

Having a cow

After giving birth, cows *lactate* (produce milk) naturally for 10 months, and the composition of their milk works well for most cheese styles. Cow's milk ranges from deep to light, creamy yellow, depending on what the animal is eating and its breed.

Cow's milk is comparable to goat's in terms of fat and protein content. Its composition is different, however, and that affects how cheese is made. In general, cow's milk has a medium weight in the mouth, somewhere between goat's milk (the lightest) and sheep's milk (the richest).

Getting your goat

Like cows, goats lactate for about 10 months after giving birth. Bright-white goat's milk and cheese are usually described as having a citrus-like tang, which is the result of the milk's chemistry.

Although goat's milk has about the same fat and protein content as cow's milk, its fat globules are generally smaller, and its chemical composition makes it easier to digest. It's ideal for many people who have problems consuming dairy products (see the "Lactose intolerance" sidebar).

Feeling sheepish

Sheep require a lush grass environment to be profitable dairy producers. They produce milk for the least amount of time — about six to seven months after giving birth — and their milk is quite different from both cow and goat's milk, with far more fat and protein.

Like goats, sheep produce milk that is white in color (rather than yellow) because they convert the carotene in what they eat into vitamin A. Not surprisingly, sheep's milk and sheep's milk cheeses often taste like the smell of a clean wool sweater.

Smart starter

Whatever type of milk is used, the first step in cheesemaking is to heat the milk to a specific temperature (see the "To pasteurize or not to pasteurize?" sidebar in this chapter). While it's heating, the cheesemaker adds a *starter culture*, which acidifies the milk, beginning the coagulation process. It works by fermenting the *lactose* (natural sugar) in the milk and converting it to lactic acid.

Acidification can happen naturally (think of that past-its-expiration-date carton in the back of your fridge), but it needs to occur in a controlled manner for a cheese to develop as the cheesemaker intends.

While acidification is happening, several other important things take place, including the onset of flavor production and the restriction of unwanted bacteria. Desired yeast, mold, and bacteria can also be added to the milk, which has a further impact on the taste and style of the cheese. (See "Exploring Cheese Styles," later in this chapter.) Because of the presence of these organisms, cheese is a living thing, even after it's been aged. Kept whole, it will continue to ripen, even after you take it home. (For storage tips to keep your cheese at its best if you can't eat it right way, go to Chapter 4.)

Curd is the word

After the milk has been acidified, it's ready to be *coagulated*, or turned into *curds* (soft clumps of the protein casein) and *whey* (a liquid byproduct). The cheesemaker makes curds by adding *rennet*, an enzyme that occurs naturally in the stomach lining of mammals, to the acidified milk.

Fluid milk can be coagulated through acidification alone, and this is indeed how some soft, fresh cheeses are made (see Chapter 2 for details). The traditional coagulant, however, is rennet.

Lactose intolerance

Chances are you or someone you know has issues tolerating milk or other dairy products (Laurel does!). Although some people do have true dairy allergies, most often the problem is *lactose intolerance*, which is the inability to digest significant amounts of *lactose*, the natural sugar in milk.

The problem comes from a shortage of the enzyme *lactase* in the gut, which naturally breaks down lactose so it can be absorbed into the bloodstream. People without enough lactase experience uncomfortable gastrointestinal symptoms after eating foods with lactose.

Fortunately, most cheeses have little lactose because it has been converted to lactic acid. In general, the longer a cheese is aged, the less lactose it contains, and certain types of milk, like goat's, contain less lactose and are more easily tolerated by the intolerant. Digestive aids such as Lactaid can also help ease the symptoms of lactose intolerance.

 Many cheesemakers now use non-animal rennet made from microbial and yeast-derived coagulants or thistle. These are sometimes referred to as "vegetarian" rennet. Check with your cheesemonger about rennet types if you have a dietary preference.

Curd is considered fresh cheese and can be eaten as is (while sitting on a tuffet, perhaps?) or made into specific shapes and styles (check out Chapter 2).

From curd to cheese

After the curds have formed, the cheesemaker really gets down to business. The curds are scooped up and ladled into perforated molds that will determine the final shape of the cheese. Shapes are usually wheels, *boules* (slightly flattened balls), cylinders, discs, squares or pyramids for some goat cheeses.

The molds also permit the whey to drain out, removing excess moisture from the curd. Other ways exist to expel moisture after the curd has drained, including cutting, salting, stirring and cooking the curd, and pressing down on the cheese itself.

To pasteurize or not to pasteurize?

Pasteurization is the process of heating milk to inactivate or kill certain types of bad bacteria, such as E. coli or listeria. The United States practices *batch* or *vat pasteurization*, in which milk is heated to 143 degrees Fahrenheit for at least 30 minutes, or *HTST* (high temperature short time), in which milk is heated to a minimum of 161 degrees Fahrenheit for at least 15 seconds. All mass-produced, "industrial" milk and cheese in the United States is pasteurized, but some states do permit the sale of *raw* (unpasteurized) fluid milk.

Milk must be heated to make cheese, so the term *raw milk cheese* is a misnomer. In the United States, it refers to cheese that has been heated to a lower temperature (*thermalization*, which is 131 degrees Fahrenheit, for between two to 16 seconds), which still destroys certain bad bacteria, while preserving many of the flavor complexities within the milk and resulting cheese. The cheese must then be aged for a minimum of 60 days before it is legal to sell. Importing raw milk cheeses aged less than 60 days is illegal.

Raw milk and cheese are high-demand specialty products. Proponents believe that raw milk tastes better, is more digestible, and helps boost the immune system. They also believe pasteurization destroys the beneficial bacteria and enzymes that lend flavor and complexity.

The greatest debate currently raging between the FDA (U.S. Food and Drug Administration) and much of the domestic cheesemaking community is over the production and sale of raw milk cheese. In the European Union, raw milk cheese aged less than 60 days (such as Brie or Camembert; see Chapter 2) is legal to sell for consumption, but Australia and New Zealand have regulations similar to the United States.

The controversy is generally over the "inherently dangerous" nature of raw milk versus pasteurized product. If raw milk or cheese is contaminated by certain bacteria, it can harm or even be fatal to infants, young children, the elderly, or those with compromised immune systems. Although this is a valid concern, pasteurization doesn't guarantee product safety. Whether milk is raw or pasteurized, safety comes down to sanitation measures, dairy herd health, production practices, and proper shipping and storage.

Moisture content is important in cheesemaking, because it ultimately determines whether a cheese will be soft (Chapter 2), or hard (Chapter 3). To transform curd into different cheeses, the addition or natural growth of yeast, mold, and bacteria is also usually required (with the exception of some fresh cheeses). These organisms will affect the taste and style of the final product. (See "Exploring Cheese Styles," later in this chapter.)

Worth its salt

After the cheesemaker drains the curd, he or she applies salt in the form of a *brine* (saltwater solution) or exterior dry-rub. Salt serves several important purposes, the most important of which is enhancing flavor. Salt can also keep unwanted organisms away from the cheese; however, it can also inhibit the growth of bacteria that are essential to the final product. In all instances, salt draws out more moisture so the outside of the cheese — the *rind* — will form.

Ripe for the picking

Ripening a cheese correctly and determining when it is ready to eat takes experience. That requires understanding the milk, cheese recipe, style, and how to adjust the environment where the cheese is aged.

In Europe, ripening is often done by an *affineur*, someone who is trained in *affinage*, or finishing a cheese. In the United States, it's usually done by the cheesemaker and, in some cases, the cheesemonger.

Depending on the milk and style of cheese, moisture content in cheese is either desirable or problematic. If the cheese is meant to be hard and aged longer, like Parmigiano Reggiano, then more whey needs to be removed. If it's going to be a soft, gooey cheese like Camembert, more moisture is necessary. (See Chapters 2 and 3 for details on soft and hard cheeses.)

Exploring Cheese Styles

In the previous section, we describe the basic process by which all cheese is made. But every style of cheese has its special characteristics and properties. These are developed by making specific adjustments during the cheesemaking process. Here, we discuss what makes one cheese different from another.

Getting cultured: Bacteria and mold

Besides the starter culture, which acidifies the milk (refer to "Making Cheese," earlier in this chapter), other ripening agents such as bacteria, mold, and yeast are usually added during the cheesemaking process. These will affect the flavor and texture of the cheese.

Although you've probably been taught to be afraid of bacteria and mold, the environment has many indigenous, harmless, and even beneficial bacteria and molds. Without them, many cheeses you know and love wouldn't exist because the original cheese styles were derived from specific molds growing organically where the cheeses were made or aged (such as a natural cave; Roquefort is a classic example). Some "good" molds and bacteria include the following:

- Blue veins in blue cheeses
- White mold on Brie
- Orange-red rind on "stinky" cheeses
- Holes inside Swiss-style ("alpine" or "mountain-style") cheeses

---

Digging deeper into cheese online

The Web is home to some great cheese resources. Check out the following:

- ✔ **The American Cheese Society** (www.cheesesociety.org): A professional industry organization that is also open to consumers.

- ✔ **Cheese Chick** (www.cheese-chick.com): A Web site offering various online resources for cheese enthusiasts.

- ✔ **Culture: the word on cheese** (www.culturecheesemag.com): Yes, that's us, but we're not shy! Culture's online library profiles an extensive compendium of cheese varieties, compiled by our team of experts.

Rinding your business

The rind of a cheese is its skin, and it protects the cheese so it can age. On certain cheeses, such as washed rinds or soft-ripened, the rind is the actual mold that ripens and flavors the entire wheel, making it crucial to the end product.

Here are the main rind categories:

- ✔ **Natural:** These cheeses are exposed to air and their rinds are formed as part of the drying-out process. This will happen naturally on all cheeses if left to themselves, without the addition of bacteria or mold to the milk or curd (see Chapter 3).

- ✔ **Soft-ripened (or bloomy):** Softer cheeses like Brie can have a white, "bloomy" rind that literally ripens the cheese from the outside in. This happens because of a specific mold. The rind is edible and imparts a mushroomy flavor. (See Chapter 2 for a closer look at these cheeses.)

✔ **Surface-ripened:** Similar to soft-ripened bloomy cheeses because they ripen from the outside in, rinds on these cheeses are particularly wrinkly with a tangy, floral taste (see Chapter 2).

✔ **Washed:** Salt brine, wine, beer, and spirits are all used to "wash" various cheeses so specific bacteria form and flourish, resulting in a "stinky" cheese. The rind is usually reddish and sticky with a distinct odor. The interior is less intense-smelling and, when aged, will become soft and gooey with meaty, yeasty flavors. (See Chapter 2 for some of our favorite washed rind cheeses.)

✔ **Waxed:** This isn't the same wax used for candles. Rather, it's a special, non-edible cheese wax that remains flexible over time. It protects the cheese, allowing it to age without cracking, and inhibits unwanted molds from growing (see Chapter 3).

Chapter 2

A Hard Look at Soft Cheeses

• •

• •

Soft cheeses aren't just for timid palates, despite their often-delicate texture and higher moisture content. Whether you serve them solo, or use them for cooking or as a garnish, their variously milky, oozy, gooey, spreadable, fluffy, salty, stretchy, or stinky characteristics command attention. In this chapter, we introduce you to the main categories of soft cheese, so you can get beyond the bland stereotype.

Soften Up

We confess we have a, uh, soft spot for this category of cheeses. Their beauty lies in their seeming simplicity. Soft cheeses are generally meant for eating as-is, and

are only enhanced by the addition of an accompani-
ment or two — and yes, a glass of wine or beer counts!

 Consume soft cheeses within a week or two of
buying them, tops. Their lack of aging, moisture content (which can provide a breeding
ground for bad bacteria or mold), and low salt
content (with the exception of soft brined and
pressed cheeses) aren't conducive to a long
shelf life. If they smell sour or have spots of
bluish-green or pinkish-red mold, toss them.

Soft cheeses fall roughly into five categories, which we
explore throughout this chapter: fresh, semi-soft, soft-
ripened, washed rind, and blue. Don't be intimidated
by the variety; becoming familiar with soft cheese is
just a matter of learning their basic rind types and textures. Which, of course, means eating lots of cheese.

Fresh

If you've ever had fresh cottage cheese or mozzarella —
the kind that comes packed in water or brine, rather
than entombed in plastic — you've already sampled
fresh cheese. The style simply refers to cheeses that
have not been aged.

Five categories of fresh cheese exist: soft, whey, brined
or pressed, non-melting, and *pasta filata*. In the sections that follow, we provide more detail on each type,
and recommend a few specific cheeses for you to
sample.

Soft

Soft cheeses are sweet, creamy, milky, or tangy.
Texturally, they may be in loose, clumpy curds or

velvety smooth; fluffy and airy; satiny or somewhat runny; squeaky, crumbly, or moist; dry, grainy, or chalky. But all *good* fresh cheeses possess the pronounced rich, creamy, clean flavor of fresh milk. Tangy flavors are generally associated with cheeses made from goat's milk (refer to Chapter 1).

Some of the most notable soft cheeses include the following:

- ✓ **Chèvre:** *Chèvre* is the French word for goat. It usually refers to soft young cheese that is the consistency of cream cheese. It makes a great savory addition crumbled on pizzas, salads, and sandwiches, and pasta, egg, vegetable, and grain dishes.

- ✓ **Cottage cheese:** At once tangy and sweet, with rich, clumpy curds, this cheese is usually made from cow's milk.

- ✓ **Cream cheese:** Artisanal cream cheese is made by using a starter culture and coagulant. It's not as rich or heavy as mascarpone because it's made from a combination of milk and cream. Its flavor is more tangy and sour than sweet.

- ✓ **Mascarpone:** This Italian *triple-crème* (intensely rich cheeses made by tripling the amount of cream used during the cheesemaking process) is satiny, sweet, and thick, but spreadable. It's an essential ingredient in the classic dessert tiramisu.

These cheeses are best enjoyed with fresh fruit; spread over good-quality toasted bread; or (if you're like us) eaten shamelessly by the spoonful.

Whey

These cheeses are made from the residual solids left in whey after it's reheated at a higher temperature (refer to Chapter 1 for more about whey). They're smooth and supple, or fluffy and moist. Most often white-to-ivory colored, these cheeses should have a fresh, milky smell — never sour. Their flavor may range from mild and sweet to tangy or sour.

Here's a look at two of the most popular cheeses made from whey:

- ✔ **Gjetost:** This Norwegian goat/cow's milk snacking cheese is the exception to other whey cheeses. It's cooked for a long time to produce a sweet-tasting cheese with a caramelly flavor and slightly sour finish. It's a deep butterscotch color, with a fudgy texture.

- ✔ **Ricotta:** The most common whey cheese, ricotta has a fluffy texture and sweet, milky flavor. It may be made from cow, sheep, or water buffalo milk. It's wonderful for baking, in pasta dishes, or with fresh fruit.

Brined and pressed

Brining means a cheese is soaked in an acidified salt-water solution to inhibit bacterial growth (basically, it's a preservation method from the days before refrigeration). That's why brined cheese in bulk is still stored in its liquid. Packaged fetas are sealed in plastic so they won't oxidize and develop (bad) bacteria and mold.

Brined cheeses are creamy to crumbly. Many pressed cheeses are brined as well as dry-salted to extract moisture, which gives them their dry, crumbly, or hard texture. Others are simply dry-salted. All of these cheeses can be made from whole milk or whey.

The most popular varieties include the following:

✔ **Cotija:** This Mexican cow's milk cheese ranges from moist to dry and very crumbly, or is hard and used for grating. It's used in many traditional dishes including soups, salads, beans, and *antojitos* (fried masa dough snacks).

✔ **Feta:** The most ubiquitous of brined cheeses is native to Greece, but other countries such as Bulgaria, France, and Israel also produce feta. Although traditionally made from sheep or goat's milk, many producers include cow's milk, to keep costs down.

✔ **Ricotta salata:** Unlike fresh ricotta, this cow or sheep's milk cheese is firm to hard and used for grating or shaving over food.

 Brined and pressed cheeses are salty and are best used for cooking. They add a zesty flavor to salads, grain or vegetable dishes, or pasta.

Non-melting

Cheese that doesn't melt? How is this so? It's because of its acidity level, which affects the chemical composition of the cheese. Cheeses that are either very high or low in acid don't melt. Most in this category are of a definitive ethnic origin (Greek, Indian, Mexican), and have specific applications in their respective cuisines:

✔ **Haloumi:** This firm, semi-dry Cypriot (from Cyprus; although it is also made in Greece) goat or sheep's milk cheese is traditionally served as a snack or dessert. Fried Haloumi drizzled with honey is a delicious treat; dredge it lightly in flour before cooking.

✔ **Paneer:** Dairy doesn't really play a large role in Indian cuisine, with the exception of this firm, bland, unsalted, acid-set cheese. It is used in curries and other saucy, savory dishes, or in desserts that are often soaked in flavored simple syrups, such as rosewater.

✔ **Queso blanco:** A soft, mild Mexican cow's milk cheese that is creamy to dry and crumbly in texture. It is used as a filling or garnish in a variety of savory dishes. It is an *acid-coagulated* (or acid-set) cheese, meaning that vinegar, lemon juice, or another acidic ingredient is used to set the curd, rather than rennet.

 Non-melting cheeses are ideal if you're looking for something that retains its shape on the grill or in a sauté pan, or as a textural garnish for soups, salads, curries, or stews.

Pasta filata

Pasta filata ("stretched curd") cheeses have an elastic, sometimes chewy texture, and are usually a striking white color. Some varieties are brined or smoked. A hot-water bath at the curd stage makes them pliable, so they can be stretched into the desired shape.

You'll enjoy chewing on any of these:

✔ **Burrata:** This Puglian Italian cheese hit the U.S. radar less than a decade ago, and is now in great demand (and made domestically, due to its perishability). You can see why: It's a combination of mozzarella and cream. Slice through the edible exterior skin and you'll be rewarded with an intensely rich, milky filling. Serve as you would mozzarella, or with fresh summer fruit, such as berries.

✔ **Mozzarella:** A good-quality fresh mozzarella is a thing of beauty: sweet, rich, and delicate. It's usually made from water buffalo or cow's milk, and is a traditional specialty of Campagna, Italy. The best way to enjoy mozzarella is to eat it just after it's been stretched. Fresh will turn you off the rubbery packaged stuff forever. Great for sandwiches, pizza, or cubed into pasta.

✔ **String cheese:** Children love this mild, ivory-colored cow's milk snacking cheese. Many stores also carry pure-white Armenian string cheese, which often has black nigella seeds added for a touch of pungency and visual appeal. It is traditionally made from sheep or goat's milk, and braided.

Semi-Soft

Semi-soft cheeses have a smooth, slightly moist surface and texture. They may or may not have tiny *eyes* (holes), and their *paste* (interior) is white, ivory, or pale-yellow to gold or orange in color. As the name implies, they're not totally soft: you can't put your finger through them (not that *you'd* do that, of course!).

Creamy and buttery

Texture and rich, full flavor, which has a distinct buttery quality, unite the cheeses in this group. They may have waxed or natural rinds. They're classic table cheeses, meaning they're often served before or after a meal, but they're far more versatile than that! Here are two of our favorites:

- ✔ **Havarti:** This popular Danish cheese has a fairly soft texture, small eyes, and a buttery flavor with a tangy finish.
- ✔ **Port Salut:** This mild French cow's milk cheese has an ivory to pale-yellow interior, and distinctive orange rind.

 Creamy semi-soft cheeses love fruit, fresh or dried. They also go well with cured meats, as long as they're not too heavily spiced or fatty. You can also use them at the table and for melting, sandwiches, macaroni and cheese, casseroles, or snacking.

Savory and earthy

Savory just means the opposite of sweet, but cheeses with these flavor profiles tend to be described as mushroomy, musty, nutty, barnyardy, sheepy or goaty (assuming that's the milk they're made from), vegetal, grassy, or meaty. They're often rustic cheeses (frequently described as "farmhouse" style), and their rinds may be off-white, gray, tan, or yellowish, while their interiors range from pure white to bright yellow or orange.

If you're feeling adventurous, try one of these two cheeses:

- ✔ **Caerphilly:** A natural rind Welsh farmhouse cheese made with cow's milk. It has a slightly sour, white-to-ivory, crumbly paste.
- ✔ **Colby:** This American cow's milk supermarket staple is bright orange because it's colored with

annatto, a tree seed used as food dye. It's reminiscent of mild cheddar, with a faintly sour tang at the finish.

Like their creamy counterparts, savory cheeses are lovely with fruit. Most varieties are ideal for baking, melting, sandwiches, casseroles, or snacking.

Soft-Ripened

The flavor and texture of these cheeses personifies "creamy" or "buttery." The molds used in their production give them their distinctive white to pale-yellow, beige, or grayish rinds, which can be fluffy, chalky, or wrinkly in texture (*bloomy rinds* are soft-ripened cheeses). But everyone knows it's what's inside that counts, and in this case, that inside is rich and rewarding.

Surface-ripened refers to a style of soft-ripened cheese with a wrinkly rind — the result of its production and aging. A classic example is France's St. Marcellin (see "Stinky and gooey," later in this section).

Creamy and buttery

If your idea of heaven is a decadent butter-bomb of a cheese, these are for you. They all have delicate rinds that encase full-flavored, white to pale-yellow interiors that range from almost fluffy to soupy:

✔ **Brillat-Savarin:** One of the most famous triple-crèmes, this French cow's milk number with a thin, delicate rind is revered for its airy, whipped-butter consistency and mildly sweet flavor.

- ✔ **Fromager d'Affinois:** This factory-made French cow's milk *double-crème* (contains twice the amount of cream normally used in cheese production) proves that cheese doesn't have to be made by hand in small batches to be delicious. Satiny, oozy, buttery . . . this is a sure-fire crowd pleaser for a party or dessert plate.

- ✔ **St. Marcellin:** These discs of surface-ripened cow's milk cheeses from the Rhône-Alpes region of France have delightful pungency, and satiny to soupy ivory paste. When young, they're traditionally sold in little ceramic ramekins, so they can be heated before serving, if desired. They grow more pungent with age.

 These cheeses are subtle, so serving them with anything too strong or complex will overpower their delicate flavor and texture. Plain crackers or a baguette are good choices, along with fresh or dried fruit, preserves, and toasted nuts.

Savory and earthy

When a cheese is described as earthy, that's not to say you're eating the equivalent of a mouthful of soil. It just means the dominant flavor is reminiscent of what fresh, clean dirt, mushrooms, or a forest floor smells like.

Other flavors you can expect from this category include beefy, tangy, herbaceous, goaty or sheepy (depending on the milk used), or musty. If that sounds good, try:

- **Brie:** A bit more sweet, fruity, and feminine than its cousin Camembert. Like Camembert, however, some excellent domestic versions and good pasteurized imports are available.

- **Camembert:** Slightly mushroomy, with a satiny, creamy, off-white interior and edible, bloomy white rind.

- **Crottin:** These beloved little goat cheese "buttons" are a staple in France. They may be fresh, mold-ripened, or occasionally aged for up to two or three months (at which point they become a hard cheese). Unless aged, they're soft to crumbly or chalky in texture, with a pleasant tang.

Earthy soft-ripened c`heeses are excellent with fall or winter fruit such as purple grapes, apples, or pears, or dried figs, muscatels (wine grapes), or cherries. On the savory side, pair them with cured meats, on a cheese plate. Add some country-style bread and a salad of bitter greens dressed with good extra virgin olive oil and red wine vinegar, and you have a rustic but satisfying meal.

Washed Rind

For some cheese lovers, the earthy, savory cheeses we describe in the "Soft-Ripened" section are as strong as they care to get. But for others, a Camembert just doesn't cut it. These washed rind cheeses are for adventurous eaters who are fans of the funk. Their rinds are sticky and orange, reddish, pinkish, or brownish in color, with interiors semi-soft to almost soupy.

When you hear someone liken a cheese to dirty feet, socks, or armpits, or describe it as funky, yeasty, *barnyard* (with a whiff of barn, wet hay, or animal), beefy, or meaty, they're usually talking about a washed rind.

Cheese of any type should never smell like ammonia, which is a sign it's overripe. Washed rinds in particular are prone to this characteristic.

Before you decide to throw out an ammoniated cheese, give it some fresh air. Unwrap it and let it sit on the counter for an hour or so to "breathe," and then shave off the outer layer of the cut surfaces. Many times, this will do the trick if your cheese isn't too far gone.

Savory and earthy

These cheeses do emit some signature stink, yes, but their aromas can also be mushroomy, vegetal, minerally, meaty, or grassy. Their rinds may be orange, pinkish, or gray, with ivory to yellow paste. These are masculine cheeses, with their pungent odor and in-your-face, punchy flavor:

- ✔ **Liederkranz and Limburger:** Good quality versions of these German washed rind cheeses are glorious, although they are also produced in Wisconsin. They are soft, supple, and pungent (too much, for some people), with intensely rich, creamy interiors.

- ✔ **Pont l'Évêque:** A creamy, rich, pungent washed rind with a distinct beefy flavor. This ancient French cheese can be eaten as-is, or heated in a small ramekin for dipping bread. Heaven!

✔ **St. Nectaire:** A washed rind from the Auvergne region of France; dense, with a semi-soft texture, and mild barnyard overtones.

Savory stinky cheeses are as versatile as their creamy cousins. Balance their earthiness or tanginess with fruit, or serve them with salty or spicy cured meats or paté. Add a simple salad and crusty bread, and you have an easy, elegant dinner.

Stinky and gooey

Gloriously, unapologetically stinky, yet also creamy, silky, soupy, or oozy. We love these cheeses for their bold taste, but also for how they demonstrate the art of turning sweet, raw milk into something on a different level entirely.

Here are a few for the fearless:

✔ **Epoisses:** One of the crown jewels of French cheese, this seriously stinky washed rind is soupy, with a rust-colored rind. Eat it by cutting a hole in the top and spooning out the silken white interior.

✔ **Munster:** Not to be confused with the American version, spelled "Muenster," this washed rind French cheese was originally made by Alsatian monks. It has a bright-orange rind and creamy, deliciously stinky white interior.

✔ **Taleggio:** The ugly, bumpy, orangey-gray rind on this flat, square washed rind from Italy's Valtaleggio region belies its surprisingly delicate interior. Pungent but also moist, buttery, and fruity.

The difference between Brie and Camembert

These two famous French cheeses come from different places (they're known as AOC, or *Appélation d'Origine Côntrollé*, products; the designation name may vary slightly depending upon the food product or beverage). AOC regulations, which also pertain to wine, olive oil, and other artisan foods, specify manufacturing region, animal breed and husbandry, and production methods. But these two soft, bloomy rind cheeses also differ in flavor and appearance.

Brie de Meaux and Brie de Melun are raw cow's milk cheeses named after their respective towns in Île-de-France. They're shaped into flat discs a little over a foot in diameter, and weigh up to six pounds. The flavor is tangy, clean, and sometimes a bit fruity.

Camembert de Normandie is from the town of Camembert. It's a squat, raw cow's milk cheese made in small (approximately five-ounce) wheels. It has a more mushroomy, earthy flavor than Brie.

Because both cheeses are made with raw milk and aged for less than 60 days, they're illegal for export to the United States. The versions we find here have been pasteurized, and may come from a factory or small artisan producers, so the quality varies greatly.

Pair these with fresh or dried fall fruits for a dessert plate, or a loaf of rye or pumpernickel bread, grainy mustard, and cured meats and cornichons. Serve with hoppy IPA, light pilsner, lambic, or other fruity beers.

Feeling Blue

There's no gray area with blue cheeses. People either love or hate them, but we maintain that the haters just haven't been introduced to a really great blue.

Blues are made via the introduction of molds that are added to the milk at the beginning of the cheesemaking process. After the wheels have been formed, they are *needled* — pierced throughout to form tiny holes. The holes allow air into the cheese, which reacts with the enzymes and bacteria and creates the characteristic "veins" and pockets that are the hallmark of blue cheese.

Mellow blues

If the thought of blue cheese reminds you of the smell and flavor of a dirty sweat sock, give these blues a chance — they may surprise you with their creamy, slightly sweet, fruity notes:

- ✔ **Gorgonzola dolce:** Sweeter, milder, and creamier than its savory counterpart (see the next section), this young cow's milk cheese is one of the most recognizable blues around.

- ✔ **Fourme d'Ambert:** Unlike most French blues, which are powerfully assertive, this is a more sedate version with salty blue veins.

- **Maytag blue:** Made by *that* Maytag family, this American classic is sweet, crumbly, and almost waxy in texture.

- **Original blue:** California's only farmstead blue is from the milk of Holstein cows grazing on lush coastal pastures. The result is a sweet, milky blue with a beautiful white paste.

 These cheeses go great in salad or with a dessert course. Pair them with some honeycomb, toasted nuts, and sliced seasonal or dried fruit (think peaches, apples, or pears), and you have an elegant final course that will impress your guests.

Strong blues

Blues can also be described as minerally, earthy, salty, grassy, toasty, beefy, or spicy — depending on milk type, *terroir* (soil/environment), and how the cheese is made and aged.

We recommend the following strong cheeses:

- **Mountain gorgonzola and gorgonzola piccante:** Both types of this cow's milk cheese (gorgonzola dolce is a sweet, creamy version) originate from northern Italy. These are earthy, footy, or spicy versions with a dense, possibly crumbly or slightly dry paste.

- **Roquefort:** One of the world's most famous cheeses, true Roquefort is made from the milk of the Lacaune sheep and aged in the local caves. Potent, earthy, sheepy, creamy, and dreamy.

✔ **Valdeon:** A little salty, with a heady rush of earthy intensity. This Spanish cow and goat's milk cheese comes wrapped in Sycamore leaves, making it visually stunning on a cheese plate.

Enjoy these cheeses with savory accompaniments like prosciutto or other hams, and olives for a pre-dinner cheese plate, or pair them with deeply flavored dried fruit such as pears, figs, or dates.

Chapter 3

Grate Tastes: Hard Cheeses

. . . .

. . . .

*H*ard cheeses have a range of textures and styles, with an equally diverse array of flavors. Just like soft cheeses, they can be made from cow, sheep, or goat's milk. They can be dry and shard-like; crumbly, supple, smoky, stinky, grassy, sharp, mellow, earthy, tangy, or buttery; but they are extremely versatile. In this chapter, we introduce you to hard cheeses and explore the two main categories so you understand just how "grate" they are.

Hard to Beat

We need to come clean. As much as we love soft cheeses (which we praise in Chapter 2), we're just as partial to their aged cousins. Although a fresh cheese such as ricotta is more blatantly and immediately expressive of an animal's milk, some hard cheeses are the sensory equivalent of a jar of summer fruit preserves on a dreary winter's day. Hard cheeses made from peak-season milk can have intensely rich, complex flavors and colors that evoke the lush pasture the animals grazed upon at the time. They're like a cheese time capsule!

Hard cheeses are excellent for the table or on a cheese platter, but this group also boasts some of your best cooking, baking, and melting choices. That said, some hard cheeses have such stunning flavor, heating them would be a shame.

The more aged a cheese is, the less moisture it has, and the longer its shelf life. This makes hard cheese a practical and economical choice. If stored correctly (see Chapter 4 for more about storing cheese), you can keep a hunk of well-aged cheese for up to two month (although we're not sure how anyone can resist for that long!).

If a hard cheese smells sour or ammoniated, try setting it out on the counter sans wrapper to air. Use a sharp knife to shave the surface you plan to eat, and that will usually solve the problem. Just cut off or scrape away spots of blue-green or whitish mold. If the cheese still smells and tastes off — sour or astringent — chuck it.

Although soft cheeses are more varied in style, type, and production method, hard cheeses can be just as complex in flavor and texture. In this chapter, we brea hard cheeses into two main categories: semi-firm (also called semi-hard) and hard. But trust us: "Hard" doesn't mean difficult. These cheeses are easy to love.

Semi-Firm

Semi-firm cheeses may be your best friends in the kitchen. The smooth, supple texture and full, rich flavor of these cheeses make them adaptable for almost any cheesy situation. At the table; on a party tray or plate; for snacking, grating, cooking, melting, baking, or fondue, most semi-firm cheeses get the job done.

Most semi-firms range in color from ivory, beige, or pale yellow, to golden or orange. Their rinds may be made of brightly colored wax; dry and of varying shades of brown or gray; or slightly sticky or visibly mottled with black, gray, or rust splotches. Some cheeses in this category have *eyes* (holes caused by bacteria added to the milk during production, which you see most often in Alpine or Dutch cheeses).

This style is more firm than a semi-soft cheese, hence the name, but these cheeses aren't extremely hard and dry, either. What separates them from the semi-soft variety is that they've been aged, and may be labeled as such. Some, like Gouda, can range from semi-soft to semi-firm to hard cheese, depending on their age.

Any cheeses marked extra-aged, grana, *stagionato, vecchio, stravecchio*, or *piccante* are hard cheeses, which we describe in the next section.

In the following sections, we look at the various flavor profiles you find in semi-firm cheeses, and list some of the more popular cheeses in each category.

Throughout the sections, we describe some cheeses as *Alpine*. These are the most popular kind of washed rind (refer to Chapter 1) semi-hard cheeses, and as the name implies, they originate from the Alps, and may be Swiss, German, French, or Italian in origin. They have tacky rinds that are usually tan to gray in color, with smooth, ivory to butter-yellow paste. Usually made from cow's milk, alpine cheeses are smooth, slightly pungent, and nutty or buttery, but may also have grassy, oniony, beefy, or earthy characteristics. Due to the lush, high-altitude summer grass, wildflowers, and other plants the cows eat, these cheeses are a true expression of the region, although they have also inspired several American cheesemakers to produce similar versions.

Sweet and rich

Cheeses that have a sweetness to them haven't been enhanced with additives. Rather, *lactase*, the natural sugar *in* the milk (refer to Chapter 1) gives them that property. Season, type of animal/breed, what the animals have been eating, production method, and type of cheese are the other factors that influence why a cheese might have a predominantly sweet flavor, rather than nutty or tangy.

These same factors that influence the sweetness of a cheese also affect its richness, which is more pronounced and palpable in younger, softer cheeses (as opposed to a hard cheese, such as an aged cheddar). "Rich" is a characteristic of texture and flavor. It feels full on the palate; the butterfat literally coats your mouth.

ere are some of the most popular sweet, rich, semi-
rm cheeses:

✔ **Bel Paese:** Mild, buttery, and pale yellow in color,
this popular Italian cow's milk table cheese works
equally well as a melter.

✔ **Monterey Jack:** This California classic is perhaps
the most well-known (real, not processed)
American cheese. White or ivory in color, with a
smooth, creamy consistency and mild-to-slightly
sour flavor, Jack is one of the most versatile
cheeses in terms of use and preparation method:
few cheeses are better for melting. It is often flavored with aromatics such as hot peppers or
spices.

 For a summer picnic classic, serve these
cheeses with a soft white wine or rosé, paired
with fruit, a baguette, and some ham or other
mild, salty cured meat.

mooth and nutty

may seem as though most cheeses are smooth, but
ome, like Emmentaler, have a particularly supple,
lmost waxy texture, even though it's not quite as
oist as a Gruyère.

Nutty" is a taste characteristic that means the cheese
as a dominant taste (usually accompanied by odor) of
oasted or raw nuts. Some cheeses specifically have a
azelnut quality, while others are just, well, nutty.
gain, this reflects the milk and what the animals have
een eating, but it's more about the aging process,
hich reduces the moisture in a cheese, allowing the
ilk's flavor complexities to shine.

These are some of the best smooth and nutty semi-hard cheeses:

- ✔ **Emmentaler or Emmental:** Swiss cow's milk cheese in the classic sense: the smooth, almost waxy, pale-yellow paste is pocked with large holes. Emmentaler has several designations, depending on its age, but its minimum maturing time is four months.

- ✔ **Gruyère:** Perhaps the most famous of all Alpine cow's milk cheeses, this Swiss washed rind (refer to Chapter 1) beauty is complex and versatile. It has a tacky, tan-colored rind, and is sweet and nutty with oniony or meaty undertones. A good Gruyère should be cave-aged for at least nine months, and will be labeled as such.

- ✔ **Manchego:** Perhaps the most recognized Spanish cheese, this sweet, nutty sheep's milk number from La Mancha is traditionally served with *membrillo* (quince paste). Young Manchego (six months or less) is more smooth and supple, and more aged versions (usually aged 12 months) are drier with a hint of sheepiness. The rind has a distinctive herringbone pattern and is waxed.

- ✔ **Ossau-Iraty:** This regal sheep's milk cheese from the French and Basque Pyrenees is a *tomme*-style meaning it has been cave-aged. It has a pale tan natural rind, and a sweet, nutty, ivory-colored paste.

- ✔ **Comte:** This alpine cow's milk cheese hails from the Jura Mountains on the French-Swiss border. Nutty and pale yellow with a beige rind, it's eminently snackable and meltable; this is one of the most versatile cheeses around.

These are ideal cheeses for snacking, cheese plates, or sandwiches. Emmentaler and Gruyère are classic melting cheeses, most notably for fondue.

Sharp and savory

A sharp cheese has a bit of edge and bite to it. These cheeses may be described as zesty, horseradishy, or pungent, and they pack a punch — even if they're not a traditionally stinky cheese.

Here are our top picks for this category:

- **Cheddar (aged, or "sharp"):** Cheddar makes everything better! The name of this traditional cow's milk cheese refers to its place of origin (the village of Cheddar, in Somerset, England, although excellent versions are now made in the United States) and its production method, which involves *cheddaring*. This means salt is added to the curds before they are kneaded, cubed, drained of whey, and then stacked and turned. The result is a dense, flavor-packed cheese that ages from 3 to 60 months.

  For serving, melting is about the only thing cheddar doesn't excel at. As with certain non-melting soft cheeses (refer to Chapter 2), its acidity level affects the chemical composition required for it to melt.

- **Fontina:** A pungent, buttery Italian alpine cheese with a bit of bite. Like its cousin Gruyère, it's a good all-purpose cheese, but is softer in texture.

- **Provolone:** A good provolone has a bite to it, and an ivory paste. (Mass-produced versions are usually bland and rubbery.) Made from cow's milk, it's usually pear or sausage, shaped, and may also be aged until it's a hard cheese (and this produces an incredibly sharp cheese), or smoked. Originally from northern Italy, it's now produced throughout Italy and in the United States.

 All of these (except cheddar and aged provolone) are ideal melting cheeses, but they're equally at home on the table or party platters, for snacking, and in sandwiches. All hold up well for entertaining, whether they're cubed, sliced, or served in a DIY block or wedge.

Hard

Hard cheeses have a lower moisture content than soft cheeses, which is the result of how they're made and how long they're aged (sometimes up to 15 years). They have thick, tough rinds, and their interiors resemble shards or look like a craggy wall of rock; the color ranges from pale yellow to golden.

Although hard cheeses can be delicious for snacking, their true purpose is for grating over food. The most famous of these is Parmigiano Reggiano, known as the "King of Cheeses."

 Don't think that hard cheeses can't handle the heat. Use them grated atop casseroles, gratins savory bread pudding, or macaroni and cheese for a crunchy, toasty, savory garnish.

Sweet and rich

Because these cheeses are aged, the *lactase* (milk sugar) becomes more pronounced, giving them flavors of caramel or butterscotch. In the "Semi-Firm" section, we discuss how a younger, softer cheese can feel rich on the palate, but more aged cheeses can taste rich because of those same concentrated sugars. Rather than coating the mouth, a bite of cheese like an aged Gouda will explode with those sweet flavors. They may also have a slight, pleasant crunch, due to the crystallization of amino acids as the proteins in the cheese break down.

Here are two of the best sweet and rich hard cheeses:

✔ **Aged Gouda:** The longer one of these spectacular Dutch cheeses is aged, the more deep gold, caramelly, and crunchy it becomes. Like cheddar, it isn't a melting cheese.

✔ **Mimolette:** This flaming-orange French fireball has a hard, craggy, gray rind and distinctive round shape. It may look like a rock (and be about as hard to cut) when aged, but its waxy interior is smooth and sweet, with a nutty finish.

 Use these cheeses for snacking or on a cheese plate with toasted nuts, fresh apples or pears, or dense dried fruit such as figs, apricots, pears, or dates.

Granular and nutty

Because of their production style and aging, these cheeses have a flaky, shard-like, or granular consistency. When not used for grating, they're usually served with a special, spade-shaped knife designed for breaking off small chunks, which best showcases their distinct texture and gives each piece greater surface area to showcase its sweet, nutty fragrance.

What's the difference between Parmigiano Reggiano and Parmesan?

Parmigiano Reggiano is a DOP, or *Denominazione de Controllata Protetta*, cheese from Emilia-Romana (specifically, the provinces of Reggio-Emilia, Parma, Modena, and parts of Bologna and Mantua). This noble cheese — one of the finest in the world — has been produced by hand according to nearly the same methods since the Middle Ages. Parmigiano Reggiano is so valuable that some cheese storage vaults are managed by banks, which keep them as collateral for dairies to which they have provided loans.

The name Parmigiano Reggiano can only be applied to cheese made from this region, from specific breeds of cows fed a specific diet, in a specific way. To protect the product and avoid consumer confusion, all similar cheeses within the European Union and other parts of the world must be marketed as "Parmesan." Although some excellent versions exist, including Italy's Grana Padano, none have the real thing's consistency of quality or flavor.

Check out these aged cheeses:

- **Dry Jack:** This hard version of Monterey Jack can be aged up to four years on average. Its flavor changes as it ages, but it's typically mellow, salty, nutty, and rich, with earthy notes.

- **Parmigiano Reggiano:** It's revered for its nutty flavor, sweet aroma, and pale golden, granular paste flecked with white spots. Pesto, risotto, pasta, *frico* (fried or melted into a lacy disk): the uses for this famous cow's milk cheese are many.

Use these cheeses at the table or on a cheese plate with toasted nuts and fresh apples or pears, or dense dried fruit such as dried figs, apricots, pears, or dates. Both are wonderful grated on top of everything from pasta to salads.

Sharp and savory

Sheep and goat's milk cheeses in particular get more sharp and intense as they age, because the inherent qualities of the milk are only amplified as their moisture content reduces. If you love bright, pungent flavors, these are for you:

✔ **Aged Crottin:** These popular French goat cheese "buttons" are usually sold fresh or soft-ripened. When aged two to three months, they can be off-white or covered in gray to blackish-mold, but once grated, you'll be rewarded with an assertive, zesty, brilliant white interior.

✔ **Pecorino Romano:** This most famous of Italian sheep's milk cheeses is also sold younger, but when hard, it's a glorious, off-white colored grater with a thick, hard rind. It adds a sheepy, tangy punch to savory dishes, but you can also eat it with fruit — the sweetness provides a nice balance to the cheese.

All cheeses in this category add a pungent, zesty kick when grated atop savory dishes like pasta, casseroles, soups, or salads.

Chapter 4

Buying, Serving, and Storing Cheese

. . . .

. . . .

*E*ven if you're familiar with the different styles of cheese, visiting a cheese shop or cheese counter can be daunting. And even if you do make a purchase, questions may remain. What's the best way to serve the cheese? What beverage should you pair it with? How should you store leftover cheese? Fear not. In this chapter, we've got you covered.

Discovering What You Like and Don't Like

A whole world of cheese is out there, and you'd be doing yourself a disservice if you stuck to your old standbys. Be open-minded. We frequently see repeat customers buy the same cheese over and over again because they're crazy about it. Don't get us wrong: We're happy when you adore a cheese. But by trying new things, you just might discover something you love even more!

The key to broadening your horizons and finding new favorites is to figure out just what it is you like in a cheese and build on that. Take a look at Chapters 2 and 3, and identify a cheese — soft or hard — that you love. What about it appeals to you? Is it the style, milk, rind, flavor, or texture? All of these?

Now, look through the chapters, hunting out similar characteristics in other cheeses. For example, if you like the crunchiness in Parmigiano Reggiano, consider trying aged Gouda. Then comes the fun part: Tasting the new cheese.

Don't feel like you have to buy a piece of cheese without sampling it. Your cheese-monger should always let you sample before buying.

As you explore the different types of cheese, you'll build up a cheese vocabulary and establish a relation-ship with your cheesemonger. Talk to your cheesemon-ger, so he or she can turn you on to a new variety that suits your palate. When describing what you're looking for, focus on texture and just a general flavor profile, such as "sharp" or "buttery."

By following flavors instead of types, you may be pleas-antly surprised at where your adventures in cheese take you. You may think you have an aversion to blue or goat's milk cheeses or washed rinds (see Chapter 2), because of their inherent flavor characteristics and

nell. But sometimes, the way a cheese is aged or the
rpe of milk it's made from can change your percep-
on. A semi-firm goat's milk Gouda can be nutty, but-
ry, and not at all goaty, and a blue made with sheep's
ilk can be sweet, creamy, and a little bit salty, but
ee of that pungency that can be too much for some.

Serving Cheese Properly

heese is the ideal food for entertaining. It's easy to
erve and most people love it. It can be passed around
n a platter, or guests can help themselves from a
omposed plate. Serve an interesting assortment of
heeses, and you've got an instant conversation
tarter. In this section, we explore the basic elements
f serving up cheese and assembling a cheese plate.

Cutting to the chase

he way you slice a cheese can affect your enjoyment
f it. Please note that we're not referring to whole
heels (unless they're small rounds, like camembert)
r massive blocks of cheese here. Any cheese you pur-
hase will come pre-cut and wrapped, or be cut to
rder by your cheesemonger. After you get it home,
ese tips will help you get the most out of your
heese.

The number one rule is to have an equal ratio
of *paste* (interior) to rind. Resist the impulse
to excavate the interior of a cheese out from
the rind. Not only does it destroy the aesthetic
integrity of the cheese, but some people actu-
ally like to eat the rind.

The cutting edge in cheese slicing

If you're big on entertaining, you'll want to have three types of cheese knives. (Fortunately, they're often sold in a set.) Each serves a specific purpose that helps to maximize the flavor and amount of portions you'll get from a cheese. They are as follows:

- **Cheese cleaver:** This mini-version of a meat cleaver may have a pointed or flat head. It's used for slicing or breaking off shards from dense cheeses, such as aged cheddars, Goudas, or Manchego (refer to Chapter 3).

- **Cheese plane (planer):** This tool is a flat, stainless-steel triangle with a sharp-edged slot in the center. You drag the plane across the top of the cheese and it shaves off thin, even slices. A cheese plane is used for harder cheeses such as Gruyère and Grana Padano (Chapter 3).

- **Soft-cheese knife:** This knife resembles a paring knife with a gentle upwards curve. The holes punched in its blade minimizes the surface area that makes contact with the cheese. This prevents cheese from sticking to the knife as it's cut and served, making for a cleaner, more attractive slice with less waste left on the blade. Ideal for soft, creamy cheeses such as Brie, Fromager d'Affinois, or Danish Blue (Chapter 2).

Here's how to slice cheese based on its style or shape

- **Small wheels, discs, pyramids, or squares:** Positioning the knife in the center of the cheese, cut into even, wedge-like slices.

- ✔ **Wedges of soft to semi-soft cheeses:** Cut into thin slices, starting at the point of the cheese.

- ✔ **Wedges of semi-firm to hard cheeses:** Cut wedge in half lengthwise, then cut each slice into portions crosswise.

- ✔ **Logs:** Slice into even cross-sections.

- ✔ **Blue cheeses:** Slice the wedge from the center of the thin edge to equally spaced points along the thick edge.

Determining the ideal temperature

Serve cheese at room temperature. This allows the flavors to open up, so the cheese can be enjoyed at its full potential. Removing cheese from the fridge 30 minutes before serving will usually suffice, unless it's very hot in your kitchen.

Washed rind or goat cheeses grow more pungent as they warm up. If it's hot or humid, you might want to think about serving something else, or set these cheeses out a few minutes in advance.

Creating great plates

Unlike learning to cook, which takes time and repetition to achieve a level of comfort, composing a cheese plate is fast and easy, after you grasp the basics. It doesn't matter if you're dining alone or hosting a party for 100; the rules are the same, give or take a few adjustments.

In the following sections, we offer our tips on how to assemble a plate that leaves a lasting impression.

Knowing how much cheese to serve

If you're serving the cheese at a party along with other hors d'oeuvres or as a pre-dinner appetizer, allow approximately one ounce of several cheeses per person.

There are 16 ounces in a pound, so a half-pound of three cheeses will usually suffice for a dinner party of eight.

Understanding the art of composition

Serve between three to four cheeses for up to 12 guests. Any more than that can lead to palate fatigue (which is the tastebud equivalent of what happens if you smell too many perfume samples; your nose becomes immune to the complexities in each new fragrance).

When selecting the cheeses, take into account how dense or rich they are. A creamy, high-butterfat cheese will fill up your guests more quickly than something stinky, blue, or sharp, which most people will consume in smaller quantities (although this really just comes down your guests and how much they love cheese).

Whatever you select for your plate, choose cheeses that increase in intensity. Anything works: You can do all blues, sheep, or soft-ripened. Just make sure you serve them from lightest in flavor and salt to heaviest, always ending with the blue (which can obscure your palate for tasting the other cheeses).

For the most diverse, well-rounded plate, try the following (refer to Chapters 2 and 3 for specific cheese ideas)

✔ One creamy or mild cheese;

✔ One semi-soft or semi-firm cheese with a bit of bite or a washed rind or soft-ripened; and

✔ One hard or blue cheese.

 Arrange the cheeses clockwise, in order of how guests should taste them, if you're serving individual cheese plates or a plate for a small gathering. For a party situation, don't worry about the order, but label the cheeses, including where they're from, so guests know what they're eating.

 Tell your cheesemonger how many people you're entertaining. He or she will likely have a different suggestion if you say you need a cheese for a party with 20 guests, versus a picnic for two. Some cheeses aren't ideal for small portions (think of a very delicate washed rind, which will get squashed), or perhaps they only sell certain cheeses by the half-wheel or wheel (which is the case with small cheeses like Epoisses, or St. Marcellin). Conversely, an extremely expensive cheese can be affordable, if you're only purchasing an eighth of a pound.

Picking sides

One of the most frequent questions we hear from customers is, "What do I serve with this cheese?" Honing your accompaniments down to one, two, or three options can be intimidating, but avoid the temptation to turn your cheese plate into a smorgasbord. It takes away from the cheese, which, after all, is the star of the show, and can be overwhelming to the palate.

In the next two sections, we offer some simple and satisfying ideas for the two main categories of cheese plates: savory and sweet.

Savory

For a savory plate, serve a bowl of dry-cured or crunchy, briny green olives such as Picholines or Lucques — don't forget a small dish for the pits — *or* cornichons, and one or two different types of cured meat. Slice up a loaf of crusty bread and set out a little bowl of some grainy mustard. That's it!

You can also mix things up a bit for a fall or winter cheese plate. Serve cured meat with some grapes, slices of apple or pear, dried fruit, or chutney (sweet with savory), *or* pickled vegetables or a simple salad (try to incorporate a sweet element, such as citrus segments or candied nuts in the salad, to add balance).

Sweet

For a dessert plate, you can never go wrong with some beautiful seasonal fruit, especially if it's locally grown, and some toasted hazelnuts, almonds, walnuts, or pecans. If it's cold and dreary, serve thin slices of apple or pear or pomegranate seeds; dried fruit and a bit of honeycomb; or good-quality preserves with toasted nuts and slices of toasted walnut or sourdough bread.

In warmer weather, think berries, or cherries and other stonefruit such as peaches, nectarines, or plums. Served with some plain crackers or baguette, these go beautifully with soft-ripened, goat, or fresh cheeses.

 Avoid serving cut fruits that oxidize easily like apples, pears, peaches, or nectarines if you have a big party; instead, save them for a small gathering and slice right before serving.

Pared-Down Pairings: Cheese and Beverages

That wine (or beer) and cheese is a match made in heaven is no coincidence. Think of all the wine regions in major cheese-producing countries such as France, Italy, and Spain. In those cultures, wine is an everyday table beverage, not something for a fancy night out. The same is true of countries that are known for both their beer (and sometimes wine) and cheese: Germany, Switzerland, Belgium, the Netherlands, and the U.K. For non-tipplers looking for something to sip with their cheese, a wonderful selection of non-alcoholic beverages is on the market, including "dry" sodas (as opposed to sugary) flavored with everything from spices and herbs to fruit, and an ever-growing array of specialty fruit juices.

Think of pairing like a good marriage: Each person should possess his or her own, distinct, positive qualities that, when combined with their partner's, elevate the relationship to more than the sum of its parts. In other words, you may love a cheese on its own, but when matched with the right beverage, you get fireworks!

The noble grape

Wine and cheese are classic partners, but to get the pairing to really work, you need to think about matching the qualities of the wine with those of the cheese. Just because a wine is excellent and a cheese is delicious doesn't mean the two will be delectable together. Decide your priority: If you're planning to drink a specific bottle, pair the cheese to suit the wine. If you want specific cheeses, choose the wine that best complements them.

 Always think about matching intensity when pairing wine and cheese. Don't choose an overpowering wine, because that can be a waste of a great piece of cheese.

 Here's a list of time-tested combinations, with complementary intensities and attributes:

✔ Crisp white wines like Sauvignon Blanc pair best with tangy goat's milk cheeses (Chapter 2).

✔ Buttery Chardonnays are a good bet with buttery creamy cheeses (Chapter 2).

✔ Lighter red wines, such as Pinot Noir and Sangiovese, marry well with mid-weight cheeses like Gruyère and Colby (Chapter 3).

✔ Big red wines — Cabernet Sauvignon and Bordeaux blends — can stand up to an aged cheddar or another cheese with some bite and heft (Chapter 3).

 If you're ever at a loss for what to serve with a diverse group of cheeses, pick bubbles. Sparkling wines help cleanse your palate of the mouth-coating butterfat from the cheese, and don't conflict with most cheese flavors.

Hop to it

Beer and cheese can also be ideal partners. As with wine, the key is to look for matching intensities and complementary attributes.

Raise a glass to these great pairings:

- ✔ Hoppy India pale ales, light Pilsners, and lambics (fruity, effervescent beers that cleanse the palate) pair well with stinky washed rinds (see Chapter 2) that are full of big flavors and aromas.

- ✔ Wheat beers and lagers are nice with goat cheeses and soft-ripened styles (Chapter 2).

- ✔ Porter, stout, or lager are good matches for hearty Alpine cheeses, cheddar, and Gouda (Chapter 3).

- ✔ Fruity, sour lambics are a fun counterbalance to salty blues (Chapter 2).

- ✔ Light, citrusy Mexican beers are ideal with spicy, savory dishes garnished with regional cheeses like Cotija or Queso Blanco (Chapter 2).

The teetotaling table

You needn't be a wine, beer, or spirits drinker (nor an adult) to enjoy cheese with a beverage. Juices, specialty sodas, teas, or even coffee can make a great mate with cheese. Just avoid anything too sweet and cloying, which will overload your palate.

Fruit is often paired with cheese, so experiment with interesting fruit juices (many of which are available in sparkling versions):

- ✔ Pair white grape, pear, or cherry juice, or a fresh-pressed, soft apple cider with chèvre, or other fresh or soft-ripened cheeses (Chapter 2).

- ✔ "Dry" (not sweet) sodas bring out the best in washed rind, soft-ripened, or semi-firm cheeses with a rich, buttery texture (Chapter 2).

Tea and coffee can be successfully paired with cheese, too. The rules are essentially the same as for pairing wine: Match intensity and attributes. Here are some duos we like:

✔ Bright, herbaceous green teas match soft, creamy cheeses like chèvre or triple-crèmes (Chapter 2). Sweet or floral teas such as jasmine also complement these cheeses.

✔ Complex or spicy, fruity, or smoky teas like Earl Grey and Lapsang Souchong go well with blue cheeses (Chapter 2).

✔ Slightly tannic, fruity or spiced teas, like Darjeeling, do right by nutty Alpine cheeses, cheddars, and Goudas (Chapter 3).

✔ Coffee can be great with top-quality fresh cheeses such as ricotta or mascarpone, either as a component of a dessert, such as cannoli, or served in a dish with some biscotti or other cookies.

Storing Cheese Successfully

Cheese is best consumed as soon as possible after purchase (especially soft cheeses), but we understand that sometimes your eyes may be bigger than your stomach. If you need to store your stash for later, here are some tips to keep your cheese as fresh as possible.

First, try to purchase cheese cut to order, as opposed to pre-cut, wrapped, and ready to go. Freshly sliced cheese will taste better and last longer, and you can rewrap it in its original paper.

You can buy the special cheese paper used by cheesemongers, which is specially made to keep cheese fresh.

It has two layers: One is a permeable membrane that permits the cheese to breathe, and the other is similar to butcher paper and holds in moisture. You can purchase it (Formaticum is the most widely available brand) at many cheese shops or specialty food stores, as well as online.

Even if you don't have special materials, you can store different styles of cheese effectively using items you likely already have in your kitchen:

- ✔ **Fresh:** These cheeses have a very short shelf life, so eat them as soon as possible. The most important thing is to keep them from oxidizing, so keep them sealed in their original container (which may or may not contain brine), or tightly sealed in plastic wrap.

- ✔ **Semi-soft, soft-ripened, semi-hard, and washed rind:** Seal these cheeses in plastic wrap or waxed paper, and store them in a plastic container with a tight-fitting lid. Place in the humidifier/vegetable crisper drawer of your refrigerator. Because cheese continues to ripen as it ages, be sure to air out the cheese every day or so by unwrapping it, and letting it sit at room temperature for half an hour or so.

- ✔ **Blue:** Wrap blue cheese in waxed or butcher paper and store it in a plastic container with a tight-fitting lid. Place it in the humidifier/vegetable crisper drawer of your refrigerator.

HOBBIES & CRAFTS

978-0-470-28747-7

978-0-470-29112-2

Also available:

- Crochet Patterns For Dummies
  97-0-470-04555-8
- Digital Scrapbooking For Dummies
  978-0-7645-8419-0
- Knitting Patterns For Dummies
  978-0-470-04556-5

- Oil Painting For Dummies
  978-0-470-18230-7
- Quilting For Dummies
  978-0-7645-9799-2
- Sewing For Dummies
  978-047-062320-6
- Word Searches For Dummies
  978-0-470-45366-7

HOME & BUSINESS COMPUTER BASICS

978-0-470-49743-2

978-0-470-48953-6

Also available:

- Office 2010 All-in-One Desk Reference For Dummies
  978-0-470-49748-7
- Pay Per Click Search Engine Marketing For Dummies
  978-0-471-75494-7

- Search Engine Optimization For Dummies
  978-0-470-26270-2
- Web Analytics For Dummies
  978-0-470-09824-0
- Word 2010 For Dummies
  978-0-470-48772-3

INTERNET & DIGITAL MEDIA

978-0-470-44417-7   978-0-470-87871-2

Also available:

- Blogging For Dummies
  978-0-470-56556-8
- MySpace For Dummies
  978-0-470-27555-9

- The Internet For Dummies
  978-0-470-56095-2
- Twitter For Dummies
  978-0-470-76879-2
- YouTube For Dummies
  978-0-470-14925-6